SQL: ALL IN ONE COURSE

Learn It All in 14 Days! For Beginner To Expert

SECOND EDITION

Fatima Garin

© 2016

©Copyright 2016

Disclaimer

a different timeframe to fully incorporate new information. Neither this book, nor any of the author's books constitute a promise that the reader will learn anything within a certain timeframe.

SQL: ALL IN ONE COURSE

Table of Content

Introduction

SQL is a dialect that is intended to work with databases. What are databases? All things considered, they're a gathering of information that is sorted out into a semi-unmistakable shape. However, what great does that information do on the off chance that you need to deal with it each time that you have to get to information? That is the thing that SQL does. It helps you to oversee and sort information with negligible exertion.

It has additionally saturated practically every feature of the web and, now and again, remote innovation that doesn't require any human consideration or connection for upkeep. From Facebook to Google to TV, SQL is a standard dialect in spite of the deviations from practically every company that offers it.

In this book, will cover the expansive nuts and bolts of SQL, the history, what it is, its uses, and a few contrasting options to SQL that are basic and phenomenal. There will likewise be a lexicon for you to utilize when you select the course that you might want to use to really learn SQL. This book will guide you to assets for you to learn SQL on the grounds that learning on the web through an assets that will give you practices before scrutinizing you and letting you know what you fouled up before attempting to right it I accept is a superior approach to learn something like this. A book, despite the fact that a to a great degree great asset won't offer that and during a time of innovation that offers this capacity, it would be absurd not to utilize it.

Kindly know that when learning SQL that you may need to stop and learn no less than one other coding languages like Python, Ruby, JavaScript or C+ keeping in mind the end goal to hone and see precisely what you're instructing the dialect to do. This will just truly become possibly the most important factor when you begin selecting where you'd get a kick out of the chance to take in the dialect, and it will be expressed on the off chance that you have to know another dialect in the educational area about the dialect.

Likewise, similar to all dialects, SQL will set aside some opportunity to learn and get it. Try not to be reluctant to request offer assistance. There are various spots where you can go to request help, albeit, a portion of the assets might be particular to a specific variety of SQL. As we will cover in this book, there are various SQL varieties that make learning one specific form of this dialect illogical.

What is SQL?

Keeping in mind the end goal to have a general comprehension of what SQL is, you have to realize what a database is, the manner by which it works, and how it works with SQL. Also, keeping in mind the end goal to comprehend what a database is, you have to realize what information is and what control SQL needs to control it.

Information, in a wide sense, are truths identified with something. So information about you would be your name, weight, age, eye shading, or hair shading, among various different things. In the advanced world, pictures, records, PDFs, and reports, for instance, are considered information. Be that as it may, the information can be amazingly arbitrary and look bad until it is sorted out somehow, as in a database.

With the information being composed into a database, information administration turns out to be significantly less demanding for individuals to handle and persistently redesign. The association of the information is done through a database administration framework (DBMS), which is a program that takes into consideration the control of information, getting to the information, speaking to the information, and controls database access by different clients.

Database Management Systems is utilized as a part of a monstrous assortment of ventures. For instance, Facebook needs to utilize Database Management Systems keeping in mind the end goal to store, control, and present information to individuals, companions, different exercises, and messages, among various different themes. An online telephone directory needs to store information identified with names, telephone numbers, and addresses, among others. The businesses that utilization Database Management Systems are incalculable.

Inside Database Management Systems, and as it's advanced, there are four distinct sorts of it, Navigational, Relational, SQL, and Object Oriented. There are two sorts of Navigational Database Management Systems, Hierarchical (has a parent/tyke relationship and can be imagined like a tree with every order spreading out a tad bit increasingly and is to a great degree exceptional to discover) and Network Database Management Systems (known the same number of to numerous and brings about an amazingly convoluted structure).

In the Relational Database Management Systems, everything is characterized by a table. The many to many structure found in the Network Database

SQL: ALL IN ONE COURSE

Management Systems isn't bolstered in the Relational model because of the way that there are predefined information sorts that work with it, making it one of the more prominent types of information administration today. Protest Oriented Relation Database Management Systems concentrates on tolerating new information, which is as articles with properties.

SQL is Structured Query Language and can be affirmed with each letter independently or as "See-Quel". It is the standard dialect for Relational Database Management Systems and considers somebody to pursuit, overhaul, embed, or erase database records, among others. In spite of the fact that the past rundown is quite standard for what SQL can do, it doesn't confine the abilities that the dialect offers. For instance, SQL advances and keep up databases for a begin.

There are various different sorts of SQL, similar to Oracle, MS SQL Server, MySQL, and Sybase, among others that have a tendency to take after the same SQL language structure. Notwithstanding, some of these dialects do utilize an alternate sentence structure that might be restrictive (is held and utilized by one particular organization).

SQL has various points of interest over different models of database administration, such as giving an anticipated execution, simple adaptability with no downtime, business progression, and information assurance, all with no organization.

For individuals who make their own particular sites, frequently through a webhosting administration, individuals don't have to stress over making their own particular SQL database since it will be made and kept up by the webhosting administration. Knowing regardless of whether you'll have to make a SQL will likewise rely on upon what sort of site will make, from that point, you'll have to comprehend what sort of SQL you'll have to make.

History

SQL can follow its underlying foundations back to Dr. Edward Frank Codd's distributed paper called "A Relational Model for Large Shared Data Banks" from 1970. The paper examined better approaches to structure the information inside databases and prompted to the most widely recognized type of database association utilized today, Relational Database Management Systems.

While the paper was being composed, Donald D. Chamberlin and Raymond F. Boyce from IBM were chipping away at building up another dialect referred to as Specifying Queries As Relational Expressions (SQUARE). The dialect concentrated on utilizing predicate arithmetic and a set hypothesis to choose the information asked for from the database. In spite of the fact that the dialect depended on a to a great degree thick numerical dialect, it turned into a demonstrating ground for various ideas that would then become possibly the most important factor for database administration. In 1974, Chamberlin and Boyce distributed their own paper called "Continuation: A Structured English Query Language". Continuation refined SQUARE and started investigating information recovery. In spite of the fact that SEQUEL was similarly as intense as SQUARE, yet was less demanding to peruse and utilized a more direct documentation that was simpler to keep up.

In the end, the vowels were dropped from SEQUEL and the dialect got to be distinctly known as SQL, generally because of a trademark on SEQUEL by the Hawker Siddeley Aircraft Company. The dialect, because of the facilitate that non-specialists could utilize, moved rapidly towards turning into the standard in light of the fact that would permit clients to determine the "what" instead of the "how", which was normal for a basic dialect (otherwise called a procedural dialect).

By the late 1980s, unmistakably SQL was turning into the standard for the business. Be that as it may, the dialect varieties between the execution of the dialect between real sellers was bringing about difficult issues and required a standard to be set up.

The American National Standards Institute National Committee on Information Technology Standards H2 Technical Committee on Database (ANSI NCITS H2 TCD) supported SQL in 1986 and took into account the International Standard Organization (ISO) to likewise go up against SQL as its standard in 1987. In 1989, a reconsidered standard (generally known as SQL89) was discharged.

SQL89 is otherwise called SQL1 and is considered rather useless. Significant business sellers couldn't concede to usage points of interest thus they were set apart as deficient or set apart as implementer-characterized.

1992 saw a total update of SQL89 and brought about SQL92 (or SQL2). SQL89 was utilized as a reason for the standard, however the American National Standards Institute (ANSI) took it and cut off various shortcomings and holes while introducing calculated elements to the dialect. The modifications surpassed the capacities of all the Relational Database Management Systems accessible at the time. The models set up by SQL92 turned out five circumstances longer than SQL89 and added three levels of conformance to the dialect. Section level conformance stayed basically unaltered from SQL89, the distinctions just kept a round view and connected subqueries. At the middle level, significant upgrades became possibly the most important factor, for instance, the naming of limitations, case and cast expressions, dynamic SQL, and inherent join administrators for a begin. Full-level conformance likewise got an emotional redesign with various propelled highlights like deferrable limitations, attestations, impermanent neighborhood table, and benefits on character sets and areas, among others.

Conformance testing was finished by the United States Government Department of Commerce's National Institute of Standards and Technology (NIST). In view of the testing, all sellers conformed to the standard because of an early law go in the 1990s that required a Relational Database Management Systems to breeze through government tests keeping in mind the end goal to be considered by an elected office. Be that as it may, in 1996, this testing project was disbanded with the administration refering to high expenses and now institutionalization is left to Relational Database Management Systems sellers themselves, prompting to various merchant particular elements and nonstandard executions of standard elements.

SQL99 (SQL3) started its improvement around a similar time that SQL92 was formally embraced. Created with the direction of ANSI and ISO, SQL99 is extraordinarily perplexing with a more than one thousand, five hundred page report to portray the standard while SQL92 had an insignificant six hundred pages. In 1999, SQL99 was formally discharged by ANSI and ISO and permitted development on conventional social information models. First off, SQL99 considers the consolidation of items and complex information sorts inside the social table alongside all the bolster required and permits them to work with the greater part of the OO dialects, on top of the various elements.

SQL: ALL IN ONE COURSE

There have additionally been various later endeavors to institutionalize the dialect, however not the greater part of the Vendor dialect agree to the most recent institutionalizations. The greater part of the sellers meet the prerequisites of SQL92, however after that, the dialects change uncontrollably in what precisely the dialect can do and what certain parts of the dialect remain for, similar to the scan terms and markers for the dialect.

Uses

The employments of SQL shift generally on which variant will utilize. Also, there are a wide assortment of SQL dialects running from MySQL to PostgreSQL to SQLlitethat all change how the dialect functions.

The Basics

Create – You can utilize SQL to place information into tables

Read – You can utilize SQL to inquiry recover information from a table

Update – You can modify the information that is as of now in a table

Delete – You can expel information from the table

Together, these are altogether known as CRUD and frame the reason for everything that SQL can do in light of the fact that the dialect works particularly with databases.

Manage Permissions – You can control who can get to the database and what they can see on the database

Assortments of SQL

DB2 – This is a group of Relational DATABASE MANAGEMENT SYSTEMS dialects that are controlled and keep running by IBM. IBM claims that BD2 drives the field in database piece of the overall industry and execution, yet it lingers behind Oracle in UNIX frameworks and Microsoft in Windows frameworks. It chips away at cross stages and does what a guidelines SQL dialect does and can be gotten to and worked with through various interfaces.

MSSQL – This dialect is made and keep running by Microsoft. It particularly manages web applications on the Windows stage and makes it simple to interface with databases keep running by Microsoft. It can do everything that a standard SQL dialect can do, despite the fact that it is coordinated by and controlled by Microsoft. It is conceivable that MSSQL should be paid for.

MySQL – This is a sort of social database that numerous sites use to make and after that change content to a great degree rapidly. Frequently utilized with other scripting dialects (like Python, PHP, or Perl, among others), MySQL is open source, which implies that it can be downloaded from Oracle (the organization that created it) and utilized for nothing. This specific assortment of SQL is frequently found on the web server side of a site and is normal on element pages.

SQL: ALL IN ONE COURSE

PostgreSQL – This is a question social kind of database framework. Since it is a publicly released (nobody organization controls it since software engineers from over the world have dealt with it and controlled it) kind of DATABASE MANAGEMENT SYSTEMS, the choices and confinements on what the dialect can do is practically nonexistent. It goes along and works with all principles and an assortment of lists. The scaling capacities are practically restricted as the dialect will climb and down contingent upon the information and the general population getting to the information.

Prophet – Run by the Oracle Company, the Oracle dialect runs like some other SQL dialect. It is free and can be found on the Oracle site. The Oracle dialect tends to lead in the UNIX and Linux PC universes, and has various components running from read consistency to locking instruments. Since Oracle isn't keep running by a PC particular organization, Oracle is less demanding to control and control over all stages.

Informix – Another item keep running by IBM, Informix was initially made by the Informix Corporation. IBM keeps on building up the item and centers it around the question relations DATABASE MANAGEMENT SYSTEMS. Out of the greater part of the protest connection DATABASE MANAGEMENT SYSTEMS, Informix offers various emotionally supportive networks that falls outside of the SQL standard, similar to time arrangement and uncommon extensions. Informix and DB2, despite the fact that they impart innovation to each other and are controlled by IBM, are not a similar thing and IBM has no arrangements to as of now consolidation them.

SQLite – Is another publicly released dialect, nonetheless, it is an in-process library. It is independent, server-less, zero-arrangement, and value-based database motor. Dissimilar to alternate variants of the dialect that we've secured, this one doesn't have a different procedure with regards to servers, implying that it can compose straightforwardly to consistent circle documents. One way that this specific adaptation is utilized that is greatly unprecedented is in cellphones, TVs, rambles, and so forth since it doesn't require any organization.

SQL: ALL IN ONE COURSE
The Basics

In spite of the fact that there are varieties for each rendition of SQL, there are various genuinely standard terms that are found all through every form. It would be ideal if you know the SQL isn't a case particular dialect, SELECT is precisely the same Select or select.

Language

Clauses – Components of explanations and inquiries

Expressions – Produces scalar tables and values, which is comprised of lines and sections of information

Predicates – Specify conditions, which restricts the impacts of articulations and questions or will change the stream of the program

Queries – Retrieves information in light of a given criteria

Statements – Give the broadest control, such as controlling exchanges, program stream, associations, sessions, and diagnostics. In frameworks with databases, SQL Statements will send inquiries from a customer program to a server where the database is put away before returning it to the customer, taking into account an extensive scope of brisk information control operations from straightforward contributions of information to more muddled questions.

Basic Commands

Alter Database – Modifies the database

Alter Table – Modifies a table

Create Database – Creates another database

Create Index – Creates a file (Also known as a pursuit key)

Create Table – Creates another table

Delete – Deletes information from the database

Drop Index – Deletes a file

Drop Table – Deletes a table

Select – Selects information from the database

Update – Updates information in the database

Querries

SQL: ALL IN ONE COURSE

Everything found in this segment is utilized with the Select charge that was secured under the Common Commands segment.

Distinct – Eliminates copy Data

From – Specifies the table where the inquiry will be made

Froup By – Projects pushes that have a typical esteem in a littler arrangement of lines, frequently utilized with collection works or to wipe out copy columns from an outcome set

Having – Includes a Predicate used to channel lines from the Group By statement

Order By – The best way to sort brings about SQL, if this isn't utilized, then outcomes are returned in an arbitrary request

Where – Defines the columns where hunts will be done, the various lines where the WHERE isn't valid, won't be incorporated

Administrators

= - Equal to

< > - Not equivalent to (! is additionally an adequate sign for not equivalent to)

>-Greater than

< - Less than

>= - Greater than or measure up to

<= - Less than or measure up to

As – Changes a field name when survey comes about

Between – Between a comprehensive range

Like – Match a particular character design

In – Equal to one of different conceivable qualities

Is/Is Not – Compare to invalid

Is Not Distinct From – Equal in esteem to or both are nulls

Invalid (otherwise known as Three-Valued Logic or 3VL) – Introduced to handle missing data in the social model. Utilized particularly with the Where Clause to locate the "Valid" in a table. It additionally will likewise perceive an obscure into the condition, acquiring Three-Valued Logic, which we won't go into

Data Manipulation

Insert – Adds lines (otherwise called tuples) to a table

Delete – Removes existing table lines

Merge – Combines the information of various tables, joining Insert and Update

Upgrade – Modifies existing table lines

Data Definition

Alter – Modifies the structure of a current question in different ways

Drop – Deletes a object / question in a database

Create – Creates a object / question
Truncate – Deletes all information from a table rapidly, it erases the information inside a table, not the table itself

Data Types

Character(n)/Char(n) – settled width n-character string

Character Varying(n)/VarChar(n) – variable-width string with a greatest size of n-characters

National Character(n)/(NChar(n) – settled width string supporting a worldwide character set

National Character Varying(n)/NVarChar(n) – variable width NChar string

Bit(n) – exhibit of n bits

Bit Varying(n) – exhibit of up to n bits

Date – Date values

Time – Time values

Time with Time Zone/TimeTZ – Same as Time, however incorporates insights about the Time Zone

Timestamp – Date and Time together in one variable

Timestamp with Time Zone/TimestampTZ – Same as Timestamp, yet incorporates insights about the Time Zone

Concede – Authorizes no less than one client to play out an operation or an arrangement of operation on a protest

Revoke – Eliminates a give

SQL Alternatives

In spite of the fact that SQL is a to a great degree mainstream database administration framework, there are various individuals that question its use, finding the dialect excessively troublesome, making it impossible to ace or is considered too out of information to truly be much utilize. This has prompted to a NoSQL development, albeit a few people just like to utilize different dialects.

ActiveRecord – This dialect works with the programming dialect Ruby. In particular, this dialect makes up the Model in a Model-View-Controller Paradigm. It makes, stores, and uses business protests whose information requires steady stockpiling in a database. It fills in as a part of the Object Relational Mapping framework. The dialect was presented by Martin Fowler in Patterns of Enterprise Application Architetchure.

CLSQL – This dialect works particularly with Common Lisp. Made in 2001 by Kevin Rosenburg, this dialect functions admirably with various other SQL dialects. Initially, CLSQL was intensely based off of MaiSQL (another dialect made by Pierre R. Mai). At the point when onShore Development was surrendered, the dialect was ported into CLSQL.

Datalog – This is an explanatory rationale programming dialect. As a rule, it's utilized as an inquiry dialect as a part of deductive databases, in spite of the fact that as of late, it's been utilized for information reconciliation, data extraction, organizing, security, distributed computing, and program investigation. Despite the fact that Datalog started with rationale programming, it isolated in 1977 with the assistance of Jack Minker and Herve Gallaire when they sorted out a rationale and database workshop. This dialect works with the greater part of the significant programming dialects.

HaskellDB – This is a database that works with Haskell. It takes into account unequivocal presentations of diagram for elements and fields, a question monad, and an extremely basic record framework for substances and fields. It works with an assortment of various dialects, and takes after a nearby arrangement with Active Record. It additionally works amazingly well in Ruby as a programming dialect.

IBM Business System 12 – As one of the main completely social database administration frameworks, Business System 12 vanished decently fast after it was made and discharged to the world in 1982, most likely in light of the fact that SQL turned into the received standard. Nonetheless, this dialect left a stamp through ISBL, which is another inquiry dialect that was created by IBM's UK group. The Business System 12 group rejecte SQL on the grounds that they thought it was excessively convoluted and was unsound.

Dialect Integrated Query (LINQ) – This is a Microsoft based dialect that adds questioning capacities to .NET Languages. It gives the dialects more extensive capacities by adding inquiry abilities to them, which are to a great degree like SQL explanations. The capacities of the dialects are sufficiently extended to permit them to concentrate and process information effectively from various sources. It likewise accompanies various technique names that decipher familiar style inquiry expressions into real expressions.

NoSQL (non SQL or non social) – This is, in an extremely wide feeling of the word, a kind of SQL. This form is speedier and less difficult than conventional SQL and has permitted Google and Facebook to utilize it significantly more than customary SQL. In any case, in view of an emphasis on speed and a slight change in idea to an in the end hub, the outcomes that are come back to the searcher might be off base or may not be redesigned. This information stockpiling position likewise doesn't depend on conventional, table-based social databases, rather giving its own particular stockpiling and information recovery framework.

ScalaQL – This dialect is still during the time spent being created for standard ordinary utilize. This dialect hopes to union program and database inquiries through this one dialect and depends on a decisive style to discover and decide select parts of the langue. This dialect will likewise hope to take after the style of Microsoft's LINQ dialect and utilizations Ferry (a question dialect). A total type of the dialect is still being worked on, yet data can be discovered web based investigating the current model.

XQuery – This dialect bargains particularly in information in the XML organize or in dialects that are, near it. The structure of this dialect has a tendency to take after an extremely organized, tree-like configuration with settling capacities. Everything in this dialect rises to an esteem, with the script making the expression and the expression making the outcome esteem in the dialect. Yet, the outcome esteem doesn't state how the outcome should be assessed.

Keep in mind, SQL is as of now the most mainstream database support dialect in presence at this moment, despite the fact that it has been encountering pushback from NoSQL. Knowing these different dialects won't hurt you, in spite of the fact that it will be presumably be to a great degree extraordinary that you will really utilize these dialects consistently, similar to you will with SQL.

Where to Learn SQL

There are various free assets that you can go to keeping in mind the end goal to learn SQL, however not every one of them are the same, a few assets are free while others are costly, or they require an installment to open more propelled substance while permitting you to hone on some on their less demanding substance.

W3Schools – This is a totally free learning administration that will show you how to control information in the majority of the major SQL dialects from MySQL to DB2 for nothing. The lessons are straightforward rapidly permits you go in and control information without downloading anything to your PC. W3Schools works towards covering amateurs to the most developed of information software engineers. Additionally, in case you're occupied with getting affirmed in other codes, W3Schools will offer the tests for nothing.

Vertabelo Academy – This Company offers three courses in SQL, one over Queries, Operating Data, and Creating Tables. In any case, it appears just as just a single course is free before you're compelled to pay for it and you need to have a record to do the courses. This site is additionally adapted towards amateurs.

Code Academy – Geared particularly towards apprentices, Code Academy offers a free and a paid course in SQL coding. The course itself ought to just take around three hours and will particularly let you know what you can access through the free trial and through the star arrange. This additionally will consequently let you know what you're fouling up on the site as you work with it since you'll be taking every necessary step on the site itself and not all alone PC.

Khan Academy – This is a free site and offers courses for fledglings and the more propelled level developers. As you work on the site, you will see recordings to show you and you will see what you're dealing with as you travel through the course. As you write on the left half of your screen, the consequence of what you're taking a shot freely show up on the correct side of the screen.

SQLZOO – Another free site, SQL Zoo looks towards preparing you in the greater part of the dialect varieties that exist in SQL, running from the SQL server to Oracle to MySQL to DB2 to PostgreSQL. This site begins from the nuts and bolts and works its way up, working like Khan Academy and Code Academy to demonstrate to you the outcomes as you travel through the courses. Toward the end of each area, there are tests for you to use so as to ensure that you're holding the data that the site is attempting to show you. Once you've traveled through the course, there are assets accessible as you travel through more propelled courses or your own particular SQL database administration.

Udacity – Not adapted towards a genuine programming learner, determining in the requirements segment that it's a smart thought to know Python since that is the thing that the activities are situated in. The course is additionally attempted to take a more extended timeframe, running for around four weeks in the event that you take a shot at it six hours a week. There are various activities that generally turned out to one a week, in the event that you take after the prescribed timetable. The lesson itself is free and depends on a teacher video to really show you what you're attempting to find out about. The greater part of the learning and practice will be done on the site for the lesson.

Evantotuts – This instructional exercise is precisely what it sounds like, an exceptionally wide instructional exercise that will show you the broadest terms for figuring out how to start in MySQL. For this instructional exercise, you should download WAMP for a Windows PC and MAMP for a Mac (ensure that you know how to get the summon line dealing with the program before you start). This instructional exercise is totally free and you should simply take after alongside the gave case, ensuring that your case matches what is given in the instructional exercise. Once you've completed the instructional exercise, you may need to either hone all alone or go to a site that show you while demonstrating to you any missteps to ensure you really got what you were realizing.

Udemy – Udemy offers an assortment of courses from individuals who have involvement in the business and will show you everything that they know. The web index that they offer will let you know whether the course is free, despite the fact that you may need to agree to the site, and how exceedingly appraised it is. Every one of the courses will likewise let you know what level the course is outfitted towards, so ensure that you focus on the posting, or breaking point your hunt choices. A portion of the instructional exercises will likewise offer tests, so you have the choice to maintain a strategic distance from that if taking tests isn't something that you'd get a kick out of the chance to do. Pick the instructional exercises from the Udemy seek that interests you the most, however ensure that you can really handle it first.

MySQL Tutorial – Before you even start with this site, you'll have various things to download to help with the instructional exercise that you'd be taking. Everything that you download will be particularly utilized just for this instructional exercise and will help you to complete along screenshots in every segment of the site. In any case, the instructional exercise itself is free and covers

35

information control and information definition, on top of the most fundamental meanings of what SQL is. Once you've completed the fundamental SQL instructional exercise, you can then proceed onward to utilizing SQL with an assortment of various programming dialects.

SQLCourse.Com – Another free instructional exercise that utilizations a bigger number of words than cases to show all of you about SQL. However, there are still various activities for you to do at the base of every segment for you to finish and work out in the wake of perusing through the segments. In spite of the fact that, to some degree, it might feel as if you're staggering through indiscriminately while doing the activities, everything is outfitted towards helping you. The criticism from the site is practically quick after you hit enter and will help you learn much more. In case you're intrigued and need to keep gaining from this site, there is additionally SQLCourse2.com that will proceed with your SQL instruction.

Schemaverse - Once you feel as if you're a tad bit more OK with SQL, however need to end up distinctly more agreeable, there's Schemaverse. This is an amusement that is space-construct and depends altogether with respect to PostgreSQL. While playing, you will finish against different players and once your armada is sufficiently solid, you can work towards making an AI and let the armada run itself while you unwind. Know however, this diversion may set aside a great deal of time for you to make sense of, yet there are various assets accessible on the site to help you figure out how to play.

GalaXQL – This is a SQL instructional exercise as a free web amusement. There is a virtual instructor inside the amusement that will help you experience and find out about SQL and how it functions. At whatever point you commit an error, the educator will work to make sense of what missteps you made and how to keep them from happening once more. There are various in-diversion controls that you can make while playing the amusement that will help you to comprehend what you're relied upon to do and where to find them in the reference zone on the amusement. It would be ideal if you know that on the off chance that you choose to run with this alternative, the first occasion when you dispatch the amusement might be moderate as it takes a shot at making and setting up its database. Likewise, in case you're running a Mac, the diversion may seem broken for reasons unknown, the creator of the site incorporates proposals on the most proficient method to settle the issue and move past it.

EssentialSQL – This is a free site that will help you to breakdown and comprehend SQL at tenderfoot and middle of the road levels. In case you're occupied with getting a MS SQL Certification, there are additionally various inquiries that the site offers to help you ponder, be that as it may, you might need to work your way through the whole site's instructional exercises before you start. With a specific end goal to locate the starting instructional exercise, you'll have to look under Getting Started under Programs and Classes. On the off chance that you need the middle of the road level class, then you can discover it under Programs and Classes. The course is free.

r/SQL – This is a decent asset to go to when you have inquiries regarding SQL, either on the programming side or in the event that you have general inquiries over the program that you're utilizing. Take after the principles posted for the discussion and it will permit you to get the data that you're looking for or to discover other individuals that are in a comparable situation that you are. Remember that you need to have a record on Reddit keeping in mind the end goal to really post on the site, however you can experience and read everything without waiting be a part.

Keep in mind, these are assets to show you and to help you learn. You can't just experience these dialects once and afterward mysteriously have it down. You have to set aside the opportunity to take a seat and practice the dialect, seeing precisely how it works and turning out to be more best in class with it, and all varieties of it. Not these assets will permit you to take in all varieties of the dialect, so you may need to look for more particular instructors that will stroll through the greater part of the varieties with you. Then again, you may need to swing to Reddit so as to realize what the dialects can do, and how the separate from each other in a more straightforward and practically identical way.

Conclusion

Once you've experienced every one of the courses that you're occupied with and you feel familiar with a greater part of the SQL dialects, you might need to take a gander at getting affirmed. Remember that a greater part of the confirmations are merchant particular, and there are a few affirmations that are particular to individuals who create business arrangements or senior IT Professionals. Microsoft has various particular confirmations while IBM offers the Certified Solutions Developer Credential. Prophet, as Microsoft is to a great degree particular in what they offer and may require that you take particular courses before sitting for the accreditation test.

Notwithstanding, know that it isn't remarkable for accreditations to change similarly as frequently as advances do and a confirmation that you just got might be rendered outdated inside a few years.

Additionally, since we secured a wide assortment of SQL choices, don't be reluctant to investigate those as they can upgrade your comprehension of databases and how they function. These different dialects and database supervisors may likewise give you a greater number of abilities than what SQL can offer without anyone else's input. Investigate them and check whether they're something that you might want to include to your collection top of your SQL affirmation.

SQL: ALL IN ONE COURSE

In any case, understanding the nuts and bolts of SQL, regardless of the possibility that you're not keen on an affirmation, will empower you to make and keep up your own particular databases effortlessly. It will empower you to work with various distinctive projects also. Remember that seeing how other programming dialects interface with SQL will help you grow your reasonable scope of database dialects.

Likewise recollect that taking in this specific dialect may take some time, in light of the fact that there are such a large number of varieties with it, and every variety may work distinctively with other programming dialects. The lexicon inside the book may help you on your learning venture and will help you as a kind of perspective manual for come back to as required.

Keep in mind, SQL is a dialect, and it can set aside a lot of time for you to lift it up, particularly as a result of the considerable number of varieties. Try not to be reluctant to set aside a decent lot of opportunity to take in the dialect or to request offer assistance. Requesting help may even open your brain to more capacities of SQL that you never at any point acknowledged existed or believed were even conceivable with the dialect. Try not to be hesitant to do your own examination on SQL, its varieties, and SQL choices.

SQL: ALL IN ONE COURSE

Programming dialects are ceaselessly advancing and data in books can leave date to a great degree rapidly. Stay up with the latest as you get into PC programming and don't be hesitant to join an assortment of PC programming sites that will help you to remain educated as things develop. Try not to be hesitant to survey the assets that are recorded beneath to audit and recover any data that may have been missed. Some of the sites additionally have places for individuals to agree to the site when they are software engineers and keep them redesigned. There are likewise a few gatherings that exist in the assets that were an awesome wellspring of data, Reddit was a phenomenal asset, alongside W3Schools, despite the fact that it wasn't a discussion.

In case you're authentic about getting into PC programming, investigate JavaScript and C+/C++, among others. There are an assortment of spots for you to visit with a specific end goal to take in these dialects.

Some of the assets that were recorded with the goal for you to take in the dialect likewise offer courses in learning other programming dialects, and on the off chance that you loved that specific site, alternate dialects might be accessible on the site, and you can proceed with your training with them. Reddit will likewise offer subreddits on other programming dialects that you can use so as to make sense of what programming dialects you might be occupied with realizing and what those dialects have the ability of doing, particularly with SQL.

Resources

"About." PostgreSQL - About. The PostgreSQL Global Development Group, 2016. Web. 20 June 2016.

"About SQLite." About SQLite. SQLite, n.d. Web. 20 June 2016.

"Appropriate Uses For SQLite." Appropriate Uses For SQLite. SQLite, n.d. Web. 20 June 2016.

"Best Online Courses | Udemy." Udemy. Udemy Inc, n.d. Web. 21 June 2016.

Bothner, Pat. "XML.com." XML.com. O'Reilly Media, n.d. Web. 22 June 2016.

"Brief History of SQL and SQL Standards." ETutorials.org. ETutorials, 2016. Web. 20 June 2016.

Brooks, Chad. "What Is SQL?" Business News Daily. Purch, 21 Jan. 2014. Web. 20 June 2016.

"CLSQL." Wikipedia. Wikimedia Foundation, n.d. Web. 22 June 2016.

Collins, Chris. "History of SQL." Chris Collins. Wordpress, 19 May 2007. Web. 20 June 2016.

"Comparison of Different SQL Implementations." Comparison of Different SQL Implementations. Troels, 2 Dec. 2014. Web. 20 June 2016.

"Datalog." Wikipedia. Wikimedia Foundation, n.d. Web. 22 June 2016.

Dones, Chris. "HaskellDB: A Long Tutorial." Chris Dones RSS. Chris Dones, n.d. Web. 22 June 2016.

SQL: ALL IN ONE COURSE

Dybka, Patrycja. "18+ Best Online Resources for Learning SQL and Database Concepts." Vertabelo. E-Point SA, 17 Feb. 2016. Web. 19 June 2016.

"EssentialSQL - Get Started Learning SQL Today!" Essential SQL. Easy Computer Academy, n.d. Web. 21 June 2016.

Guru99com. "What Is Database & SQL?" YouTube. YouTube, 12 July 2013. Web. 20 June 2016.

Guzel, Burak. "SQL for Beginners." Code Envato Tuts+. Envanto Pty. Ltd, 16 Dec. 2009. Web. 21 June 2016.

Hansson, David. "Guides.rubyonrails.org." Active Record Basics. Ruby on Rails, n.d. Web. 22 June 2016.

"IBM Business System 12." Wikipedia. Wikimedia Foundation, n.d. Web. 22 June 2016.

"IBM Informix." Wikipedia. Wikimedia Foundation, n.d. Web. 20 June 2016.

"Intro to Relational Databases | Udacity." Intro to Relational Databases. Udacity, n.d. Web. 20 June 2016.

"Intro to SQL: Getting Started with Databases." Khan Academy. Khan Academy, n.d. Web. 20 June 2016.

Komppa, Jari. "GalaXQL - Interactive SQL Tutorial." Www.iki.fi/sol. N.p., 3 Mar. 2015. Web. 21 June 2016.

Kurhekar, Shantanu. "What Is SQL Database? Introduction to SQL Database." What Is SQL Database? Intro to SQL Database. Microsoft Azure, 23 May 2016. Web. 20 June 2016.

SQL: ALL IN ONE COURSE

"Language Integrated Query." Wikipedia. Wikimedia Foundation, n.d. Web. 22 June 2016.

"Learn SQL." Codecademy. Codecademy, n.d. Web. 20 June 2016.

"MySQL Tutorial - Learn MySQL Fast, Easy and Fun." MySQL Tutorial. MySQL Turtorial, n.d. Web. 21 June 2016.

"News and Notes on the Structured Query Language • /r/SQL." Reddit. Reddit, n.d. Web. 21 June 2016.

"NoSQL." Wikipedia. Wikimedia Foundation, n.d. Web. 22 June 2016.

"1 Introduction to the Oracle Database." Introduction to the Oracle Database. Oracle, 2016. Web. 20 June 2016.

"A Perfect Place to Learn How to Deal with Databases." Dashboard. Vertabelo, n.d. Web. 20 June 2016.

Rouse, Margaret. "What Is DB2?" SearchDataCenter. TechTarget, Sept. 2005. Web. 20 June 2016.

"ScalaQL." ScalaQL. N.p., n.d. Web. 22 June 2016.

"Schemaverse." Schemaverse. Schemaverse, n.d. Web. 21 June 2016.

Shaw, Zed A. "Introduction: Haters Gonna Hate, Or Why You Still Need SQL." Introduction: Haters Gonna Hate, Or Why You Still Need SQL. N.p., 2010. Web. 20 June 2016.

"SQL (Structured Query Language)." What Is SQL, How Does It Work and How Is It Being Used. Ntc, 2016. Web. 20 June 2016.

"SQL Syntax." SQL Syntax. W3Schools, n.d. Web. 20 June 2016.

SQL: ALL IN ONE COURSE

"SQL Tutorial." SQL Tutorial. W3Schools, n.d. Web. 20 June 2016.

"SQL Tutorial." SQLZOO. N.p., 8 Jan. 2016. Web. 20 June 2016.

"SQL." Wikipedia. Wikimedia Foundation, n.d. Web. 20 June 2016.

"What Is MS SQL?" What Is MS SQL? HostShopper, n.d. Web. 20 June 2016.

"What Is SQL and Its Current Applications to Database Management?" What Is SQL? History, Applications and Tutorials. Software Engineer Insider, 2016. Web. 20 June 2016.

"What Is SQL?" SQLCourse. IT Business Edge, n.d. Web. 21 June 2016.

www.ingramcontent.com/pod-product-compliance
Lightning Source LLC
Chambersburg PA
CBHW070904070326
40690CB00009B/1979